FEB - - 2015

WITHDRAWN

A Robbie Reader

DARIUS RUCKER

Tammy Gagne

ALTOONA PUBLIC LIBRARY
700 Eighth St. S.W.
ALTOONA, IA 50009

Mitchell Lane
PUBLISHERS

P.O. Box 196
Hockessin, Delaware 19707
Visit us on the web: www.mitchelllane.com
Comments? Email us: mitchelllane@mitchelllane.com

Copyright © 2015 by Mitchell Lane Publishers. All rights reserved. No part of this book may be reproduced without written permission from the publisher. Printed and bound in the United States of America.

Printing   1   2   3   4   5   6   7   8   9

A Robbie Reader Biography

Abigail Breslin
Adrian Peterson
Albert Einstein
Albert Pujols
Aly and AJ
Andrew Luck
AnnaSophia Robb
Ashley Tisdale
Brenda Song
Brittany Murphy
Buster Posey
Charles Schulz
Chris Johnson
Cliff Lee
Dale Earnhardt Jr.
Darius Rucker
David Archuleta
Demi Lovato
Donovan McNabb

Drake Bell & Josh Peck
Dr. Seuss
Dwayne "The Rock" Johnson
Dwyane Wade
Dylan & Cole Sprouse
Emily Osment
Hilary Duff
Jamie Lynn Spears
Jennette McCurdy
Jesse McCartney
Jimmie Johnson
Joe Flacco
Jonas Brothers
Keke Palmer
Larry Fitzgerald
LeBron James
Mia Hamm

Miguel Cabrera
Miley Cyrus
Miranda Cosgrove
Philo Farnsworth
Raven-Symoné
Robert Griffin III
Roy Halladay
Shaquille O'Neal
Story of Harley-Davidson
Sue Bird
Syd Hoff
Tiki Barber
Tim Lincecum
Tom Brady
Tony Hawk
Troy Polamalu
Victor Cruz
Victoria Justice

Library of Congress Cataloging-in-Publication Data
Gagne, Tammy.
 Darius Rucker / by Tammy Gagne.
     pages cm. — (Robbie reader)
 Includes bibliographical references and index.
 ISBN 978-1-61228-639-6 (library bound)
 1. Rucker, Darius—Juvenile literature. 2. Rock musicians—United States—Biography—Juvenile literature. 3. Hootie & the Blowfish (Musical group)—Juvenile literature. I. Title.
 ML3930.R93G36 2014
 782.42166092--dc23
 [B]
                                                                                              2014006942

eBook ISBN: 9781612286648

ABOUT THE AUTHOR: Tammy Gagne is the author of numerous books for adults and children, including *Roy Halladay* and *Buster Posey* for Mitchell Lane Publishers. She resides in northern New England with her husband and son. One of her favorite pastimes is visiting schools to speak to kids about the writing process.

PUBLISHER'S NOTE: The following story has been thoroughly researched and to the best of our knowledge represents a true story. While every possible effort has been made to ensure accuracy, the publisher will not assume liability for damages caused by inaccuracies in the data, and makes no warranty on the accuracy of the information contained herein. This story has not been authorized or endorsed by Darius Rucker.

PBP

TABLE OF CONTENTS

Chapter One
Gone Country 5

Chapter Two
I'll Stand By You 9

Chapter Three
How Do You Like Me Now? 13

Chapter Four
Goodbye Time 17

Chapter Five
When I Get Where I'm Going 21

Chronology 28
Discography 29
Find Out More 29
    Books 29
    On the Internet 29
    Works Consulted 30
Glossary 31
Index 32

Words in **bold** type can be found in the glossary.

Darius Rucker closed out the show at the forty-seventh annual Country Music Awards in Nashville, Tennessee, with his hit song "Wagon Wheel."

CHAPTER ONE

Gone Country

It had been twenty-five years since an African American artist had reached the number-one spot on the country charts. But Darius Rucker had gotten the job done. His single "Don't Think I Don't Think About It" hit number one in October of 2008. It wouldn't be his last country single, or his last number one.

The last black artist to make it to the top spot was Charley Pride in 1983. Darius was pleased with his accomplishment. He was also **humble**. He told the *Capital Gazette*, "Charley Pride is such a legend in country music, a legend in general. To be the first one in twenty-five years is just crazy. I can't explain it. Some other people have tried. I'd like to think it's just the song. Maybe it's more. I'm proud to be that

CHAPTER ONE

guy. But I don't make music for that. I wanted to make a record people wanted to listen to."

Darius's success as a country artist is also remarkable in another way. It isn't his first triumph in the music business. In the 1990s, he was the lead singer of a popular band called Hootie & the Blowfish. Many people mistakenly think that Darius *was* Hootie. But Hootie & the Blowfish was actually the name of the whole band. Together the group sold over twenty-five million albums.

Darius Rucker appeared with Charley Pride at the 2013 Country Music Hall of Fame Medallion Ceremony. They sang "Will the Circle Be Unbroken" along with other members of the Country Music Hall of Fame.

Gone Country

The band's last album was released in 2005. But Hootie & the Blowfish still have a mighty strong fan base. And its members are still on good terms. Darius even thinks that the group might get together again to perform. He insists it will only be for a short time, though. "There's one more Hootie record and tour that we're going to do," he told *Billboard* magazine in 2012. "I don't know when, because country music is my day job—it's what I want to do."

Darius Rucker (center) rehearses with Hootie & the Blowfish bandmates Dean Felber (left) and Jim Sonefeld (rear). They are shown here preparing for the 1995 MTV Video Music Awards.

Darius performed his hit song "Radio" for fans at the AT&T Plaza in Dallas, Texas, on New Year's Eve 2013.

CHAPTER TWO

I'll Stand By You

In many ways Darius Rucker seemed **destined** to become a country music singer. He was born on May 13, 1966, in Charleston, South Carolina. Even as a child, he loved country music. His mother played the music of R&B artists like Al Green and Betty Wright in the family home. And Darius enjoyed it. But he liked country musicians like Buck Owens much more. He told Parade magazine, "My oldest brother [would say], 'Man, why are you listening to that white boy music?' But my mom would tell him to leave me alone, to let me listen to what I wanted to listen to."

Darius's mother Carolyn was in charge of the Rucker household. Working as a nurse, she raised Darius and his five siblings with the help

CHAPTER TWO

of their grandmother. Carolyn's two sisters and their families lived with them sometimes, too. Darius told *Parade* magazine that their three-bedroom house was home to eighteen family members at one point. "We didn't have a lot," he remembered, "but we had everything we needed."

Darius sang in his church choir and played football at Middleton High School. He didn't

Darius Rucker (middle left) hangs out with the other Hootie & the Blowfish members, Jim Sonefeld (left), Mark Bryan (middle right), and Dean Felber (right).

see his father much. But his mother went to all of his concerts and games. Whatever he did, she was there to cheer him on.

After finishing high school, Darius went to college at the University of South Carolina. There he met Brantley Smith, Mark Bryan, and Dean Felber. In 1986 the four musicians formed a band. Jim Sonefeld replaced Brantley Smith as their drummer a few years later. The men named the band after two of their friends at school. The original Hootie was a young man who wore glasses that made him look like an owl. Another student had round, puffy cheeks. They called him Blowfish.

Carolyn wasn't happy when Darius decided to play music instead of finishing college. But she still supported his dreams. "She said, 'I hope you go back, but you know, do what you gotta do,'" Darius told *Parade*. "If I hadn't had that, I don't think I would be here right now."

Darius Rucker performs with fellow Hootie & the Blowfish band member Jim Sonefeld in Atlantic City, New Jersey.

CHAPTER THREE

How Do You Like Me Now?

After playing small shows for a few years, Hootie & the Blowfish released their first album in 1992. Called *Kootchypop*, it sold more than fifty thousand copies. This was a big number for a band that only sold its album at its own shows. Around this time, Atlantic Records became interested in the group.

In 1994, Hootie & the Blowfish released *Cracked Rear View*, the album that made the band famous. Suddenly, everyone loved this group with the strange name. **Fans** showed their love by buying that album—more than thirteen million copies of it in its first year alone.

CHAPTER THREE

But some music **critics** didn't think that the band had **talent**. Many of them gave Hootie & the Blowfish extremely poor **reviews**. Darius and the others read the critics' insulting words. But they didn't let those words bother them.

Less than a year after *Cracked Rear View's* release, the band would win some impressive awards. Hootie & the Blowfish were named

For Darius Rucker, winning awards overshadowed the harsh words of the band's critics. Here, he poses with the other members of Hootie & the Blowfish and the MTV Video Music Award they had just won for Best New Artist.

Best New Artist at both the Grammys and the MTV Video Music Awards. At the MTV event, Darius spoke to his critics about the band's success. "We'd like to thank all you guys that hate us for making people play the record just to see why you hate us so much."

A platinum album is one that has sold more than one million copies. In the 1990s, Hootie & the Blowfish released three albums. All three of them went platinum; *Cracked Rear View* went platinum sixteen times. It seemed like nothing could stop this **beloved** group.

Hootie & the Blowfish celebrated their twenty-fifth anniversary in 2010. Columbia, South Carolina, is home to the University of South Carolina, where the band met. The town honored the band by naming a street after them.

CHAPTER FOUR

Goodbye Time

Hootie & the Blowfish released their next album in 1996. *Fairweather Johnson* didn't sell as many copies as *Cracked Rear View*. But in many ways, the band was still going strong. It felt like Darius and his bandmates were everywhere. Their fans could hear them on the radio, watch them on television, and see them perform live in concert. Many people now think that **overexposure** was part of the group's **downfall**.

"I don't even listen to the radio and I was sick of us," Jim Sonefeld joked to the *Chicago Tribune* in 1999. Soon radio stations began playing less and less of Hootie & the Blowfish—and sales dropped even further. Even two years

CHAPTER FOUR

after its release, *Cracked Rear View* had been selling about 40,000 copies a week. The band's third album, *Musical Chairs*, didn't come close to these numbers. Nine months after its 1998 release, *Musical Chairs* was selling only 1,700 copies a week.

Tony Mascaro, music director of New York radio station WPLJ, saw the change as a normal one in the music business. "I don't think it's a question of the people don't like the band.

Hootie & the Blowfish seemed to be everywhere. Here, they appear at Farm Aid in Columbus, Ohio, on September 7, 2003.

Goodbye Time

People just move on to other groups and other **phenomena**, and I just think they're not the household name they used to be," he told the *Chicago Tribune*.

The band never really broke up. But they did decide to take a break. After the release of *Musical Chairs*, Darius started working on his own music. But his first R&B album, *Back to Then*, wasn't a big hit either. Hootie & the Blowfish got back together to try again. Their fourth album didn't sell very many copies. At this point some people may have believed that the group members' music **careers** were over. But Darius knew he still had something special to offer music fans. He had always liked R&B. But he loved country.

Although Darius became famous as a part of the pop group Hootie & the Blowfish, today he's known for his country music. Here he performs at California's 2013 Country Music Festival, called Stagecoach.

CHAPTER FIVE

When I Get Where I'm Going

Darius Rucker was about to try something that few African Americans had succeeded at: a career in country music. But the **genre** was where his heart was. And following his heart proved to be the doorway to his second act. "The record I wanted to make is also the record that people wanted to hear," Darius told The *Roanoke Times*. "And that's a cool thing," he added. "I just wanted to make a record that people wanted to hear. That's all I wanted to do."

Many people knew him as the lead singer of Hootie & the Blowfish. Darius was finally going to be known by his own rightful name. His first album, *Learn to Live*, sold 60,414

CHAPTER FIVE

copies its first week. Three of the album's songs reached number one. Darius even went on to win another New Artist of the Year award, this time from the Country Music Association.

When Darius won the CMA award for Best New Artist in 2009, he exuded happiness. He had worked very hard to get to this moment.

When I Get Where I'm Going

Darius performed with the popular country music trio Lady Antebellum at the 2013 CMT Music awards in Nashville, Tennessee.

Darius released a second country album in 2010. It was called *Charleston, SC 1966*, after his birthplace and year. Two more number-one songs came from this album. His newest album, *True Believers*, was released in 2013.

Today Darius also goes by another name: Dad. His wife Beth gave birth to a daughter named Daniella in 2001 and a son named Jack in 2005. Darius also has a daughter named

CHAPTER FIVE

Darius arrives at the 2013 Country Music Hall of Fame Medallion Ceremony with his wife and family. From left to right, daughter Daniella, wife Beth, son Jack, Darius, and their guest Henry Drew.

Cary from an earlier relationship. She was born in 1995. When it comes to his singing, the kids can be about as kind as those early critics. He told *Parade* magazine, "I've never had one of my kids say, 'Sing a song for me.' If I start singing, it's always, 'Whoa—you don't have to sing! We're good.'"

Luckily his country fans can't get enough of his singing. In addition to playing concerts with popular artists like Brad Paisley, Darius also sings for **charity**. He started the "Darius

When I Get Where I'm Going

Darius Rucker poses with his wife Beth after winning the award for Best Country Solo Performance for "Wagon Wheel" at the Grammy Awards on January 26, 2014.

CHAPTER FIVE

Even though Darius Rucker has a busy music career, he makes time to help kids in need. The yearly Hootie Homegrown Round Up program gives school supplies and haircuts to children in South Carolina. Here, Darius Rucker hands out backpacks.

and Friends," concert and golf event, which raises money for St. Jude Children's Research Hospital every year. He also works with a group known as Musicians on Call. With this charity, Darius travels to hospitals and performs live for patients right in their rooms.

"It's all been so incredible," Darius told *The Frederick News-Post.* "Nobody ever gets second chances in this business. Everything has been amazing."

CHRONOLOGY

1966 — Darius Rucker is born on May 13 in Charleston, SC.

1986 — Darius forms Hootie & the Blowfish with Brantley Smith, Mark Bryan, and Dean Felber.

1992 — Hootie & the Blowfish release *Kootchypop*.

1994 — Hootie & the Blowfish release *Cracked Rear View*; it sells thirteen million copies.

1995 — Hootie & the Blowfish win awards for Best New Artist at both the Grammys and the MTV Video Music Awards. Darius's first daughter Carolyn is born.

1996 — Hootie & the Blowfish releases *Fairweather Johnson*. It is the number-one album in its first week on the charts.

2000 — Darius marries wife Beth.

2001 — Darius's daughter Daniella is born.

2002 — Darius releases his first R&B solo album.

2005 — Darius's son Jack is born.

2008 — Darius releases his first country album.

"Don't Think I Don't Think About It" hits number one on the country music charts.

Darius wins the award for New Artist of the Year from the Country Music Association.

2010 — Darius holds the first "Darius and Friends" concert and golf event to help St. Jude Children's Research Hospital.

2013 — Darius releases his third country album, *True Believers*.

2014 — Darius wins an award for Best Country Solo Performance for "Wagon Wheel" at the Grammy Awards.

DISCOGRAPHY

1994	*Cracked Rear View* (Hootie & the Blowfish)
1996	*Fairweather Johnson* (Hootie & the Blowfish)
1998	*Musical Chairs* (Hootie & the Blowfish)
2002	*Back to Then*
2003	*Hootie & the Blowfish* (Hootie & the Blowfish)
2005	*Looking for Lucky* (Hootie & the Blowfish)
2008	*Learn to Live*
2010	*Charleston, SC 1966*
2013	*True Believers*

  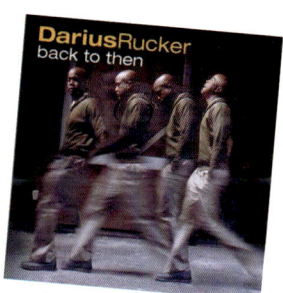

FIND OUT MORE

Books
Bertholf, Bret. *The Long Gone Lonesome History of Country Music.* New York: Little, Brown Books for Young Readers, 2007.

On the Internet
Darius Rucker
   http://www.dariusrucker.com/

Darius Rucker's Official YouTube Channel
   http://www.youtube.com/user/dariusrucker

Hootie & the Blowfish
   http://www.hootie.com/

FIND OUT MORE

Works Consulted

Biography.com. "Darius Rucker." http://www.biography.com/people/darius-rucker-224910?page=1

Boot Staff. "Darius and Friends Benefit Raises Big Money for St. Jude." The Boot, June 13, 2013.

Dauphin, Chuck. "Hootie & the Blowfish to Record Again." *Billboard*, July 27, 2012. http://www.billboard.com/articles/news/480756/hootie-the-blowfish-to-record-again

Dickens, Tad. "Darius Rucker." *Roanoke Times*, January 27, 2009.

Fischer, Blair R. "Hootie-d Out." *Chicago Tribune*, June 10, 1999. http://articles.chicagotribune.com/1999-06-10/features/9906100121_1_fairweather-johnson-hootie-rusty-harmon

Hendrickson, Matt. "Darius Rucker Is on the Right Course." *Parade*, June 13, 2013.

Hootie & the Blowfish: History. "Darius." http://www.hootie.com/internal.asp?name=Site&catID=21214&parentID=21210

McGuire, Colin. "Darius Rucker." *Frederick News-Post*, September 22, 2011.

Musicians on Call. "NBC Nightly News Features Darius Rucker, Randy Houser, and Musicians on Call 'Making a Difference.'" February 19, 2013. http://www.musiciansoncall.org/site/News2?page=NewsArticle&id=5701

Tarradell, Mario. "Darius Rucker Finds Success in Country." *Capital Gazette*, October 17, 2008.

TVGuide.com. "Darius Rucker: Biography." http://www.tvguide.com/celebrities/darius-rucker/bio/230187

Willman, Chris. "Darius Rucker on Golf, Kids, and Making the Grade in Country." *Parade*, June 12, 2011.

Wooten, Frank. "Rucker Rises to Challenge from Critics." *The Post and Courier*, September 10, 1995.

GLOSSARY

beloved (bih-LUHV-id)—Someone or something that is loved a lot.

career (kuh-REER)—The work a person does in his or her life.

charity (CHAR-i-tee)—Work a person does without being paid, or money a person gives, to help other people. Also, a group that was formed in order to do charity work.

critic (KRIT-ik)—A person who tries something (listens to music, for example), in order to tell other people whether they think it is good or not.

destined (DES-tind)—Something that happens later, but was meant to happen from the beginning.

downfall (DOUN-fall)—The failure of someone or something that was successful before.

fan—A person who likes a certain famous person, group, team, or show.

genre (ZHAHN-ruh)—A type or style of music, such as country, rock, or pop.

humble (HUHM-buhl)—A person who does not believe they are better than other people.

overexposure (oh-ver-ik-SPOH-zher)—Being seen or heard too much, so that people are not interested anymore.

phenomena (fi-NOM-uh-nuh)—People or things that are great or very different.

review (ri-VYOO)—A report that a critic gives to tell their opinion about something.

talent (TAL-uhnt)—A special ability to do something that most people cannot do well.

PHOTO CREDITS: Cover, p. 1—Jason Merritt/Getty Images; p. 4—Wade Payne/Invision/AP; pp. 6, 24—Jason Davis/Getty Images; p. 7—AP Photo/Bebeto Matthews; p. 8—EEA/ZOJ WENN Photos/Newscom; p. 10—Marion Curtis/DMI/Time Life Pictures/Getty Images; p. 12—Tom Briglia/FilmMagic/Getty Images; p. 14—AP Photo/Bebeto Matthews; p. 15—Streeter Lecka/Getty Images; p. 16—AP Photo/Mary Ann Chastain; p. 18—Ebet Roberts/Redferns/Getty Images; p. 19—Trae Patton/NBC via Getty Images; p. 20—Kevin Winter/Getty Images for Stagecoach; p. 22—AP Photo/Josh Anderson; p. 23—Michael Loccisano/WireImage/Getty Images; p. 25—Paul Buck/EPA/Newscom; p. 26—Richard Ellis/Getty Images; p. 27—Rick Diamond/Getty Images. Every effort has been made to locate all copyright holders of materials used in this book. Any errors or omissions will be corrected in future editions of the book.

INDEX

albums
    Back to Then 19
    Charleston, SC 1966 23
    Cracked Rear View 13–15, 17–18
    Fairweather Johnson 17
    Kootchypop 13
    Learn to Live 21, 22
    Musical Chairs 18–19
    True Believers 23
Atlantic Records 13
Bryan, Mark 11
charts 5, 23
CMT Music Awards 23
concerts 11, 17, 24, 27
Country Music Association 4, 22
Country Music Hall of Fame Medallion Ceremony 6, 24
critics 14–15, 24
Darius and Friends 27
"Don't Think I Don't Think About It" 5–6
Farm Aid 18
Felber, Dean 11
Grammys 15, 25
Green, Al 9
Hootie & the Blowfish 6–7, 10, 11, 12, 13–15, 16, 17–19, 21
Hootie Homegrown Round Up 26
Lady Antebellum 23
Middleton High School 10

MTV Video Music Awards 14–15
Musicians on Call 27
Owens, Buck 9
Paisley, Brad 24
Phillips, Cary (daughter) 23–24
Pride, Charley 5, 6
R&B music 9, 19
Rucker, Beth (wife) 23–24, 25
Rucker, Carolyn (mother) 9–11
Rucker, Daniella (daughter) 23–24
Rucker, Darius
    aunts 10
    awards 14–15, 22, 25
    birth 9
    charity 26–27
    childhood 9–11
    choir 10
    football 10
    grandmother 10
    school 10–11
    siblings 10
    solo career 5–6, 19–27
Rucker, Jack (son) 23–24
Smith, Brantley 11
Sonefield, Jim 11, 17
Stagecoach 20
St. Jude Children's Research Hospital 27
University of South Carolina 11
Wright, Betty 9